The Lunchtime Physician Entrepreneur

The Lunchtime Physician Entrepreneur

AN EASY BLUEPRINT FOR MOVING FROM EMPLOYEE
TO PRIVATE PRACTITIONER IN YOUR SPARE TIME!

Dr. Shanicka Scarbrough

THE LUNCHTIME PHYSICIAN ENTREPRENEUR
Published by Purposely Created Publishing Group™
Copyright © 2017 Shanicka Scarbrough

All rights reserved.

No part of this book may be reproduced, distributed or transmitted in any form by any means, graphics, electronics, or mechanical, including photocopy, recording, taping, or by any information storage or retrieval system, without permission in writing from the publisher, except in the case of reprints in the context of reviews, quotes, or references.

Unless otherwise indicated, scripture quotations are from the Holy Bible, King James Version. All rights reserved.

Printed in the United States of America
ISBN: 978-1-947054-00-4

Special discounts are available on bulk quantity purchases by book clubs, associations and special interest groups. For details email: sales@publishyourgift.com or call (888) 949-6228.

For information logon to:
www.PublishYourGift.com

Dedication

To my mother, Paulette, you have pushed me into my purpose, without saying one word.

Table of Contents

Introduction 1

Chapter 1:
My Story 3

Chapter 2:
The Physician Entrepreneur Mindset 9

Chapter 3:
Write the Vision, Make It Plain! 27

Chapter 4:
Steps to a Strong Foundation 45

Chapter 5:
How To Get Paid 61

Chapter 6:
Practice Management 79

Chapter 7:
Invest in Yourself 91

About the Author 107

Introduction

Are you on the verge of burnout in your current position as a physician? Is your vision of what it would be like to be a doctor crumbling right before your eyes? Have you thought about giving up your career after working so hard to get here? Before you throw in the towel, there's a solution.

What if you can serve your patients in a high-quality practice, without sacrificing the freedom and income you desire? What would it be like to actually feel joy, instead of dread, when going to work in the morning?

Hi, I am Doctor Shanicka Scarbrough, Board Certified Family Medicine Physician, also affectionately known as America's Favorite Family Doctor. I am licensed to practice medicine in 15 states and serve individuals across the United States as a health expert and coach. I was the successful owner and Chief Medical Officer of Divine Aesthetics Medspa Wellness Centre located in Chicago, Illinois, the private practice I started fresh out of residency after working one year in corporate medicine. I closed this practice in August of 2016 because of getting married to my husband, Pastor Darryl Scarbrough, and moving across the country to California. In the next couple of years, we look forward to opening a medical clinic as a mission of the church to service those less fortunate and without adequate health insurance.

I have also had the pleasure of creating a step-by-step six-week training program called "The Lunchtime Physician Entrepreneur E-course," which was created to physicians, such as yourself, to build their own thriving practice in their spare time. This book is the culmination of those modules into one easy book that you can read and implement at your leisure!

I created this course because I know from firsthand experience how difficult it is as a startup business to convince banks or capital investors to invest in your dream. I know the frustration of feeling like a workhorse, helping to build someone else's dream. I took the time to invest in myself, and now I want to empower other physicians to do the same thing for themselves.

CHAPTER 1

My Story

Truth be told, many of us, when contemplating the field of medicine, had some type of vision of what the practice of medicine would look like. Prior to entering our respective fields, we were all wearing rose-colored glasses, and everything is beautiful when you are looking through rose-colored glasses, right? Well let's put them back on, and let's rediscover what we can see with them, ok? Got 'em on? Good, now think back to when you first realized you wanted to be a doctor.

What did you think it would be like? In today's society, physicians are glamorized in movies, TV programs, and reality shows, like Grey's Anatomy and Married To Medicine, respectively. They are hot in the action, every moment requiring the word "STAT", saving lives everyday. Physicians, through our rose-colored glasses, are revered by the community. We are imagined to live fabulous lives, have beautiful expansive homes, drive expensive luxury vehicles, and travel around the world without a care in the world. Now, this may be the case for some physicians, especially if you are in the higher-paid sub-specialties, but this may not be the reality for most, like primary care physicians. Most of us, instead, have loans the size of the house note reflected in our rose-colored glasses!

Once you graduated from residency, took your first job, and the glasses came off, did that picture change or remain the same? For me, the picture was drastically different. When searching for a position, I knew that I wanted to work with a disadvantaged community that had difficulty accessing proper healthcare, and be a part of a team of providers that was able to make a difference in that community. Many of our minority primary care physicians, such as myself, chose the path of working at a federally qualified health center ("FQHC") for many valid reasons. I talked myself into taking a position at an FQHC in Chicago as my first job right out of residency training. The biggest draw for me was the option to enroll in the National Health Service Corps for debt relief. But once I started working there, I realized that my dream of what it meant to be a doctor looked very different from my reality.

Granted, the FQHC served as a vehicle for me to fulfill my altruistic nature to give back to my community, but that quickly wore off as the waiting rooms continued to fill with disgruntled patients who were tired of sitting, waiting for hours to be seen by a physician. I was seeing 30+ patients a day, and not feeling as though I was providing optimal care in this setting. In addition, with the increase in clerical work that became the sole responsibility of the doctor, with no time to get it done, and no raise in pay, I was beginning to feel like the walls were closing in.

Nine months into my new career, I walked into the doors of the clinic as I would any other day, sat down at my desk, and randomly without warning, I just burst into tears. I was so unhappy; I was on the verge of a nervous breakdown! How could this be? I loved medicine, I loved the patient population, and my patients loved me. Yet, the weight of each day was pushing me closer towards depression with thoughts of patient resentment, while I hid behind my smile and cheery disposition from day-to-day.

As the tears ran down my face, I made the decision that day that I loved myself more than this job, and my well-being was at stake. The very next day, I put in my letter of resignation. I was one week shy of submitting my application for the Federal Loan Repayment Program. I knew, however, that if I signed on that dotted line, I was stuck there at the FQHC for the next 2-3 years. I couldn't bear it; the loan repayment incentive was just not enough to keep me there.

Did you know that 6 out of 10 physicians said they would quit if they could? This was revealed in a survey commissioned by the Physician Foundation in 2012. A round study for the American Medical Association last year found that nearly half of the surveyed physicians called their jobs extremely stressful. More than a quarter of those surveyed said they were either burning out, experiencing burn out symptoms that won't go away, or were completely burned out and wondering if they could go on. I found this to be true in a small online study I conducted myself. 71% of physicians I surveyed stated that they had considered changing careers. That's profound!

I'm sure I wasn't the first to say that I had this "love-hate" thing with working at an FQHC everyday. I loved the work, but I didn't love the stress and overwhelming feeling that came with that experience. I knew God had a better plan for me, and it was time for me to walk in my purpose. I decided to put my future in God's hands, and let Him lead me as I am embarked upon developing a practice that didn't compromise my integrity. One of which I could shape and mold into what I envisioned when I first set out to become a physician. I began building my own empire, and I did it in my spare time. I did it all during my daily lunch breaks, to be exact! That's how the title for the e-course and the title of this book were birthed.

Per my contract at the FQHC, I had to give 90-days' notice before leaving. That gave me roughly three months to formulate a plan and execute it. I left the FQHC in August of 2013, and in the same year, I opened my office in October 2013. Won't He do it? Later in this book, I will tell you exactly how I made this happen.

In less than a year, I was working full-time in my own thriving private practice. This new opportunity gave me more autonomy and the freedom to do some amazing things. My altruistic nature kicked into high gear, and I began to volunteer with multiple organizations and nonprofits, accepted speaking engagements, and appeared as a guest on multiple radio shows. I even hosted my own health and lifestyle radio show. God blessed me to be featured as a guest speaker and writer in many publications as well, including, but not limited to, *BlackDoctor.org*, *Brotha Magazine*, and *The Citizen Online News Outlet*. I now engage a multitude of social media followers, providing health education and motivation to live healthier, happier lives one plate at a time, helping individuals shift their palates, in an effort to put a dent in the health disparities that plague our nation. It has truly been an amazing ride!

I have created the freedom I craved without compromising my financial stability. I have not missed a meal, I have not missed paying a bill, and I started and ended my practice debt-free. I have never taken out a loan for capital, nor has anyone invested into my business in the three years it has been in operation. I attribute my success to the grace of God, prayers, hard work, sweat, and the support of family and friends. And yes, I had to shed some tears. I had to have the courage to step out on faith and let God do the rest. And I am here to let you know that this is doable. And guess what? I will do it again! This time around I'll be building a medical clinic as part of my husband's ministry to serve those less fortunate. The knowledge that I gained starting a medical clinic with minimal capital will serve this initiative well. God is truly amazing!

This book is jam-packed with practical information that can get you started right away. I understand that establishing a private practice as you continue to work your full-time job is a daunting task, so I've simplified the process. Specifically, this book covers the physician-entrepreneur mindset, writing the vision, business plan generation, steps to a strong foundation, how to get paid, billing and credentialing, and investing in yourself.

I am so excited about this book and the new chapter of your life that you pursuing, and I truly believe that it will be a blessing to many of you. So are you ready to begin your journey to maximize your happiness and secure your financial future? Are you ready to be the boss rather than the workhorse employee? Are you ready to enjoy being respected in your field again? Wouldn't it be nice to give back to a community in need by providing quality healthcare on your terms? I am eager to share my knowledge with each of you, and I am ready to equip you with the skills you will need to begin laying the foundation of your private practice. While this will not be easy, the end reward will definitely be worth it. This no get rich scheme; rather, it's a roadmap to success on your own terms. This book will guide you each step of the way to create your own success story. It's now time to unleash the Lunchtime Physician Entrepreneur in YOU!

CHAPTER 2

The Physician Entrepreneur Mindset

I believe anything is possible. I see opportunity when others see impossibility. I take risks, I am focused, I hustle. I know that nothing is unrealistic. I feel overwhelming love; I embrace my child-like wonder and curiosity. I take flying leaps into the unknown; I contribute to something bigger than myself. I create, I learn, I grow, I do. I believe it's never too late to start living a dream. I am an entrepreneur.

—**Author Unknown**

Welcome to the Lunchtime Physician Entrepreneur! Thank you for taking the time to invest in yourself. In this chapter, we will discover how to shift into the entrepreneur mindset. We will focus on the following:

1. Discovering your "**Why**" – which I define as the reason or purpose for pursuing private practice;

2. Transforming your mindset from employee to employer;

3. Discovering your "**When**" – which lays out your timeline for success;

4. Envisioning your ideal practice, embracing the good and eliminating the bad.

5. Self-care and support systems

Your "Why"

First, you need to identify your "WHY," which is the force that guides your purpose and passion in life. More specifically, for the purpose of this book, determining what motivates you to start your own practice. I believe this is the most important step before embarking on any life-altering decision. This will ultimately keep you focused on achieving your goals. Identifying your "why" is like focusing the sun's energy through a magnifying glass. The force that is created can ignite the objects that surround it. Intensified focus can act as a laser beam, creating light that is so powerful it can cut through steel. Diffused light, on the other hand, has little use. This is how you must look at your "why." Having a clear sense of purpose compels you to push forward, pulverizing any obstacles that you may come up against.

Let me tell you a little bit about my "why." Her name is Paulette Williams. She is my beautiful mother. At one point in time, she was vivacious, hard-working, and an entrepreneur in her own right. She is definitely the woman who keeps me motivated on a day-to-day basis. In 2006, my mother started showing signs of memory loss, difficulty concentrating, visual hallucinations, and she struggled to take care of herself. By 2009, my mother needed full assistance with everyday living, and I began taking care of her on a full-time basis. She was only 52 years old when she was diagnosed with a progressive disease called Lewy Body Dementia, and I became her guardian, handling all of her affairs.. This life change happened during my first year of family medicine residency, which prompted my decision to move in with my mother. I made the deliberate decision to keep my mother out of a nursing home. I wanted her to be at home with a loving and supportive family, enabling me to monitor her condition and make sure she received the proper care.

While I was working 80+ hours a week, with my mother now disabled and incapable of earning a living, my income had to sustain us both. I was forced to hire hourly caregivers to take care of her while I worked, before I discovered government programs that provided additional financial assistance, covering the costs of these caregivers. My mother had to be on disability for two years before she qualified for Medicare. During this period, we were drowning in medical bills. When my third year of residency rolled around, I couldn't wait to become a licensed physician so that I would be able to moonlight outside of my clinical duties to earn extra income. When

I wasn't scheduled on rotations, I took on a job with an independent company doing home visits for patients who were elderly and/or disabled. This brought in significant additional income.

With being the sole provider for a disabled parent, I am constantly in search of ways to increase and secure our financial future to ensure that she is able to continue to receive the personalized care that she does living at home with me. My mother is the epitome of my "why." She may not be able to articulate it, but I know she is proud of her baby. I strive every day to be worthy of her pride.

Shortly before closing my private practice, I took on a full-time position doing telemedicine so that I would be able to work from home so I could be with my mother. Even though life has moved me in another direction, I am so grateful for the experience to own and operate a private medical practice, and I look forward to using the same system that I am going to teach you, doing it again in the near future. So what motivates you? Is it providing a life for you and your family? Do you desire to create a legacy? Do you want to build more wealth or be financially secure? Maybe you want to lead a more fulfilling life? Do you have a role model or hero who inspires you? Or do you just want to get out of the rat race? Are you dissatisfied at your current job? Do you want to focus on life's spiritual elements? Whatever motivates you into action, this is what you should use as your fuel. When you are frustrated, remember your "why." Whenever you fail, or question your commitment, remember your "why" and try again. When you find success, big or small, celebrate your "why." Your "why" keeps you grounded, focused, and determined to achieve the unimaginable. When you feel like quitting, think about why you started in the first place and keep it moving!

Side Note

There's a book that I recommend each of you to read. It's called *E-Myth Revisited*. Full disclosure: I am of no relation to the author, nor do I receive any royalties or financial benefit for recommending this book. This is just a book that I have found to be very helpful, and I hope that you will see the value in the book as well. It's a wonderfully creative short read that truly distinguishes between working ON your business and working IN your business. The author, Michael Gerber, has said that starting your business is like writing a book: you want to create a business that says something important about you. For example, in my business, I wanted to create an environment where I knew I would thrive. I'm a very aesthetically-driven person, maybe because I'm a Libra, but I knew I wanted my patients to enter into an environment that was calming and relaxing. When you walked into my practice, you would find that it's walls were painted in warm colors, smelled of lavender, and you may have heard a little hip-hop, gospel, or jazz music playing in the background, depending on my mood. You would also find a bowl of scriptures and inspirational sayings that patients could pick up on their way out, hopefully providing them encouragement for the rest of their day. My office had ME written all over it, and I looked forward to going into my office each and every day. So how will your book read? How will you create a practice that reflects who you are?

Mindset Transformation

What exactly is an entrepreneur? Well, Webster's Dictionary defines "entrepreneur" as a person who organizes and operates a business or businesses, taking on an additional fiscal risk in order to do so. While this is a true statement, in my opinion, it does not fully grasp the essence of an entrepreneurial spirit. Entrepreneurs are visionaries, leaders, influencers, risk-takers, creatives, and innovative thinkers. It is important to include yourself in this special group of people. Your mind-shift starts now! So, when we think innovatively and act on that innovation, we are entrepreneurs endeavoring for something greater. Congratulations! Pat yourself on the back for acting.

The following are a few things that separate an employee from an employer. Employees are used to being given tasks to complete during a specific time period. Their time is usually spent executing these given assignments. An employer, conversely, sees the bigger picture. We seek desirable outcomes from the day-to-day work by quickly weeding out what works and what doesn't, in an effort to bring us closer to our ultimate goal. This process can vary significantly from person to person. It can be for short or long term goals. As physician employees, the task at hand is to evaluate and treat as many patients in a given time period, and to finish the necessary paperwork to complete those appointments. On the contrary, as a physician employer, we are constantly evolving our practice to provide an overall positive experience for the patient, from the time they step foot in to our office up until they leave. This experience includes the patient interaction outside of the clinic, including but not limited to, billing, correspondence, and follow up. For the employee, once he or she clocks out, it's game over. The job is done until it's time to do it all over again the next day. As employers, we are constantly thinking of ways to improve and grow the business, and executing new methods to determine whether they will yield a better result.

You've heard the phrase, "Think outside of the box," To be a successful entrepreneur, kick that box right out the window! There is no box. You have to go beyond what you think you are capable of doing. Goal setting is essential. You have to write down what you envision. If you commit your visions and goals to paper, studies have proven that you will be more likely to accomplish them.

Be grateful for every challenge that you face, because it is an opportunity to learn and grow from that obstacle, and you will feel all the better when you kick the challenge's butt. Furthermore, you must be willing to take a leap of faith and gamble on your own ability to be successful. Outside of your comfort zone is where all the magic happens. You must also do what you love. Just as I stated earlier in this chapter, you must create a business that you will love because the business will become your baby. And just like those real-life crumb-snatchers, you will be committed to nurturing and watching your baby grow and mature into a capable entity that will eventually function without you. Yes, I said WITHOUT you. You will have to develop your business to the point that it will run in your absence. Those lessons can be learned down the road.

I'm all about self-affirmation. If you need to get out your sticky notes like Mary-Jane Paul in the TV show *Mary-Jane* and post them everywhere like she does to remind herself of her greatness and potential, then do you! Affirm that you are courageous, victorious, and unstoppable without a doubt! Remind yourself of this every chance that you get.

Your Timeline to Success

Transitioning from a full-time employee to running your own private practice can be difficult if you do not plan your timeline for success. When I resigned from my full-time job, I had three months to plan and open my practice. In retrospect, I was probably a little nuts for moving so fast, but the drive to succeed was, and still is, almost palpable. I knew that I was unhappy, and I had to change my environment in order to preserve my sanity. I prayed, and I fasted, and I let my faith guide my God-given vision. I started building my practice in my spare time during my lunch breaks, and when my last day came, I was somewhat prepared to move forward. I say "somewhat" because you never feel completely comfortable leaving your nine-to-five with benefits to go forth into the unknown.

Three months later I opened the doors to Divine Aesthetics Medspa & Wellness Center, and I had patients already invested in me to be their private physician. At the end of this chapter, one of your actual plans will be to create your own timeline for accomplishing your goals. Don't worry about the minor details; big picture is what we will focus on. Throughout this book, we will go into details about building a strong foundation and your timeline may change throughout the process. Don't freak out, this is ok. As an entrepreneur, your timeline is ever-evolving and changing.

Visualizing Your Ideal Practice: Embracing the Good, Eliminating the Bad

As a physician employee, there were so many frustrations and headaches that motivated me to move forward with my own plans. I was seeing over 30 to 40 patients a day, double-booked as if this was how it was supposed to be. The waiting rooms were always filled with disgruntled and angry patients who would spend hours waiting to be seen. Not only were the patients not happy, but I felt as though the organization had no respect for the doctor's time because more paperwork was being left for the physician to complete with the little time that remained in his or her 8-hour work day. Furthermore, physicians were not compensated for their increased workload, and the compensation was already low compared to the national average. When I finally sat down and compared what I was making for the organization, versus what I was taking home, I knew it was time for me to go. This presented another important lesson for putting the physician-entrepreneurship mindset into practice. Take note of all of your frustrations in your current situation because these are things that you will want to change in your own practice. Your goal should be to create a favorable working environment, as well as an overall favorable patient experience. Create a practice that will make you want to come to work each day, as well as one that will have your patients wanting to return to it for their future care.

It will also be important to implement systems, processes, and workflows that help your practice run as smoothly as possible. Take note of your current work environment. This week, write down the things that actually work at your job. What systems have been put in place that make the workflow effective and efficient? No need to waste time and resources reinventing the wheel, right? Take the things you like best at your current practice, and the lessons you have learned there, and implement them into your practice.

For instance, when I was moonlighting as a home-visiting physician during residency, I enjoyed the time out of the office and the flexible hours (meaning, after normal working hours and during traditional days off). I used the lessons I learned while moonlighting and incorporated them into the vision of my ideal practice, while I was still working my full-time job. Interestingly enough, moonlighting was how I developed initial capital. I would do home visits with my private patients after I got off work at the FQHC. The first patients for my private practice were from these home visits. I alternated between home visits and seeing patients in my new clinic. This was a system that worked for me so I rolled with it.

So take time to really look hard at how your current employer is running their office, and then document these workflows in your Action Guide at the end of this chapter. I have already given you a glimpse into my private practice, illustrating how I wanted patients to feel and what experiences I wanted them to have while under my care. This is a true reflection of my personality and my core values, as a person and as a physician.

So what about you? What does your ideal practice look like? Close your eyes and visualize this. Think about the office space, your decor, and the attitudes and work ethics of your staff. Think about your ideal patient, what you want him or her to experience upon opening the doors to your practice. Write these thoughts down, detailing your vision, making it as plain as possible. Create a business that says something important about you. Ask yourself what you value most, and then have the wisdom and courage to build your life and your business around your answer.

Again, this is an ever-evolving process of envisioning growth and success. The execution of your vision will constantly change, and you will continue to develop systems and workflows that make sense for you and your practice. This is not a static process. There will always be ebbs and flows. Someone once said that if the sea was always calm, we would never build a better boat. I love that saying because it relates perfectly to the entrepreneur's constant desire to face challenges, adapt to the environment, and improve systems for continued growth.

Self-Care and Support Systems

It's also important to have a great team in your corner. Support from family and friends can complement your efforts, but do not rely on others to cheer you on. Unfortunately, not everyone will understand your vision, your drive, or even be happy for your success. You may have some friends and family members that fall by the wayside, but that is ok. God puts people in your life for a reason, and sometimes only for a season. Cling to those who truly have your back.

Find the time to de-stress and unwind. It is important to develop healthy habits, like exercising regularly, taking time for religion and spirituality, asking for help when needed, and designating time for supportive friends and family. These habits will become necessary for survival when the going gets tough. Stress management is key.

Owning your own business is time consuming, and time management, along with some self-discipline, will go a long way. There is a time and a place for everything, but of course, I am preaching to the choir because this is how we physicians got to where we are today. We tend to be the ultimate multi-taskers, continuing to focus your attention on one task at a time while truly boosting your productivity.

Taking on this entrepreneurial endeavor will shift previous learning experiences into high gear. Always remember if this is truly your dream, "failure" will come knocking on your door. And you have to find the courage not to grant it access into your home. It's how you respond to this "f"-word that determines if your story is ultimately one of success. Failure does not mean it's time to quit. Success, however, equals failure plus the determination to try again, and again, and again, and again, until something finally sticks, and then you can breathe in the sweet savor of a job well done.

Congratulations, you have completed the first chapter of the Entrepreneur Mindset! Now for a little housekeeping. Action Guides are found at the end of most chapters. Please feel free to use this a guide to visually assist you in your transition from employee to employer.

CHAPTER 2

Action Guide

The Physician Entrepreneur Mindset

1. What motivates you? What is your "WHY": _____
   _____
   _____
   _____
   _____

2. Why do you want to start your own private practice?
   _____
   _____
   _____
   _____
   _____

3. Describe your ideal practice: _____

_____

_____

_____

_____

_____

4. What would be the mission of your ideal practice? _____

_____

_____

_____

5. On a separate sheet of paper, outline your timeline for success at six months, one year, three years, and five years.

6. Make a list of systems and work flows that are effective in your current practice: _____

_____

_____

_____

_____

_____

7. Make a list of things that frustrate you in your current practice: _____

8. What do you do to de-stress and unwind? _____

9. Describe your support system: _____

CHAPTER 3

Write the Vision, Make It Plain!

In this chapter, we're going to discuss how to write your vision and make it plain. Let's jump right in!

Goals put down in writing are dreams with deadlines. Consider your business plan as the written counterpart to what you have imagined for your own private medical practice. It's one step beyond forming a vision for where you want to be in the future. You may want to make a collage of all the things you wish to see in your ideal practice, as a tangible illustration of your dream.

The business plan is a more exact, detailed explanation of your business, your goals, and provides a roadmap of when and how you plan to achieve these goals.

In this chapter, we will cover the components of the business plan. I have included the sections I feel were most helpful for me in generating a comprehensive plan that fit my business. Be aware, however, that my list is not exhaustive. There are other components that you may find useful for your own purposes. We will discuss how to form your practice's business plan's mission statement, business description, market analysis, startup budget, financial plan, marketing plan, and the executive summary.

Mission Statement

Business Plan Step One: Develop a mission statement, which is a formal summary of the aims and values of a company or organization. To begin the process of shaping your mission statement, specifically tailored for physicians, consider these questions:

- What kind of medical practice are you trying to create?
- What do you do?
- What do you stand for?
- Why do you do it?
- Do you want to make a profit, or is it enough to just make a living?
- What markets are you serving, and what benefits do you offer to them?
- Do you solve a problem for your patients? What kind of internal work environment do you want for your employees?

A mission statement is NOT a string of buzzwords without a clear message.

Here are some additional questions that you will need to answer in order to craft your mission statement. In Chapter One, The Physician Entrepreneur Mindset, you had a chance to ask yourself some key questions in order to ascertain your "why," and identify some core values that have driven you to pursue your own private practice. In the Action Plan of Chapter One, I also asked you to write down what you thought the mission of your company would be. Does it encompass some of these key questions? Have you defined what you will do, your target customer or patient, and your motivating force for beginning your entrepreneurial journey? What makes your practice unique? How do you realize your uniqueness? Have you defined how your patients' lives would be better because your practice exists? What value do you bring? This exercise may help lay some groundwork for you to create an impactful mission statement. An effective mission statement must be a clear, concise declaration about your business strategy.

As an example, let's go through Bizilla's mission statement that I found online. Their mission statement reads,

"Our mission is to help connect people who want to sell a business with people who want to buy a business. We provide business owners and brokers with flexible options for listing their businesses online. For buyers, we offer helpful tools such as our saved listings feature and customized email alerts to make finding the right business easier."

It's very clear, don't you think?

First off, the mission statement has clearly defined its target audience. This is only for potential buyers, brokers and sellers. Secondly, what does the company do? It connects these groups by providing a convenient platform to conduct business. Lastly, what problem is it solving that makes it unique, i.e. what's its Unique Selling Position or "USP"? The business provides flexible online listing options for business owners and brokers, and unique tools and features that make it easier to search for businesses that are for sale. This mission statement is clear, concise, and to the point.

Business Description

Now let's discuss the business description. The initial portion of this document should thoroughly describe your business as far as what its existence is intended to accomplish. Include any unique points about your business and the services that you are offering. This description can include the things that make your medical practice different from your competitors, or your own valuable skills that enable you to effectively run the company. Be realistic and stick to the facts. This is not the place for marketing tactics.

In the next section of your business description, identify your intended target market. An intended target market is the group of customers (or patients) that the business has decided to aim its marketing efforts, and ultimately, its products and services. What does your ideal patient, customer, or client look like? This market can be identified by location, age, gender, income, socioeconomic status, or even psycho-graphic information, including lifestyles and similar values. This target market will become important when we go into marketing strategies.

Next, identify what problem are you trying to solve and for this targeted market. It is important for your business description to discuss a need that exists in the marketplace, and how your business will meet this need. Simply stated, explain how your practice will meet the needs of your intended target market. In your industry or specialty, what do you see as lacking for potential patients? What problem do you plan to solve for them

Also included in the business description is a section on goal achievement. Include your company's goals at the end of your business description statement as well as how you plan to achieve those goals. This section doesn't need to be long, but it should contain a clear and achievable goal, as well as a clearly defined path to reach that goal. Avoid setting unascertainable goals, for example, stating you want your company to make one million dollars in profits in the first year. It is better to set reasonable goals that you can meet or exceed in the first few years.

Market Analysis

Now let's move on to the market analysis, which determines the characteristics unique to your intended target market, and analyzes this information. This market analysis will help you make decisions for your practice, especially if you are offering additional services that are not regularly covered by commercial insurance. You might obtain this information from your local chamber of commerce, or you may be able to find it at www.business.gov, which compiles information from the U.S. Census Bureau, The Department of Labor, The Department of Commerce, and others sources. You might also want to conduct your own Internet searches on these government statistics and/or commercial statistics to verify the information.

In the market analysis, provide a description of the current industry, as well as the future outlook of where the industry is headed. Include relevant industry metrics, like industry size, trends, life cycle, and projected growth. In addition, the market analysis is where you will put more detailed information about your intended target market. Here is where you will detail patient demographics, such as age, sex, location, income, as well as the psychographics that we discussed earlier. You can also explain how your practice will be in the best position to meet this intended target market's needs. You will also want to define your market size, find out who and where your competitors are located, and how much your potential patients spend annually on your product or services in this industry. You will want to provide answers to the following questions:

- How big is the potential market for your business?
- How much market share can you gain?
- What is the market share percentage and number of customers you expect to obtain in the defined geographic area?

Then there's also the competitive analysis. Define who your competitors are, and describe what these competitors excel at providing. If possible, detail the areas in which they fall short. How can your practice fill the gap that exists with the current competition? Ideally, you are going after patients whose needs aren't being met by your competitors.

Start-Up Budget and Financial Plan

You must, must, must have a financial plan. Take the time to write down all of your potential expenses to get an idea of what you will need to start your practice. Some expenses may be one-time expenses, like medical equipment and incorporation fees. Others will occur monthly, like rent and utilities. Calculate the expenses for the first 12 months of your practice's operation. You may also want to create your own spreadsheet, but regardless of how you do it, it is imperative that you determine your startup budget.

The next step in creating your business plan is to make financial projections. Here you will create income statements, balance sheets, cash flow statements, and capital expenditure budgets. Since numbers and pictures speak louder than words, you may want to consider adding graphs to your trend analysis. Once these graphs are created, they can be easily reused for future years' budgets. In your Action Guide that follows this chapter, I have provided a link to a score financial projections template that can guide you through this process in real time.

Marketing Plan

The marketing plan is the next thing you should develop. Of course, you will also need to setup a marketing budget. Determine which marketing tools you will use, including a website, social media platforms, email marketing, mobile marketing, mailed letters, advertising, word of mouth, and/or search engines. Then you need to decide how you plan on developing your brand. Next, your marketing plan will need to cover customer engagement. How can you improve your patient's experience? Will you provide loyalty programs and incentives? Marketing is the blueprint for how to create a patient base. There is no one way to approach and execute a marketing strategy. Your strategy, however, should be part of an ongoing business evaluation process, and it should be unique to your company.

Executive Summary

Finally, we made it to the executive summary. While it's the last thing that you would write, the executive summary is the first thing a reader would see in your business plan. It gives the reader a preview of what's to come in your business plan. Be aware that some investors may only read the executive summary. Accordingly, this section is definitely going to need to stand out. The executive summary is often considered the most important section of a business plan. This section briefly tells your reader where your company is, where you want to take it, and why your business idea will be successful.

The executive summary will include your mission statement, company information, and why you have decided to pursue your own practice. It will also identify the problem that your intended target market needs solved, describe the services your practice will be provide, summarize your market analysis, summarize your financial projections if you are seeking investors or bank loans, and summarize your future plans by detailing where you would like the company to go.

After all these steps have been completed, you will have a complete business plan. The business plan will contain the following documents in the following order:

- Cover page;
- Table of contents;
- Executive summary, including your mission statement;
- Business description;
- Market analysis;
- Financial plan;
- Marketing plan; and
- Appendix with your graphs and tables.

Now this is not something that I expect you to be able to complete in a week. It will still need some occasional tweaking and adjusting after completion. Think of your business plan as being fluid, as your business grows, so should your business plan. In the first year, you should be looking at your plan monthly. Then, in years two through five, you should update your business plan at least once or twice a year. Also in years two through five, you may want to consider expanding, which often requires investors and bank loans. A comprehensive business plan will absolutely come in handy when preparing presentations for these entities. Most investors and bank loans will not even look at your business without a solid financial business plan in place.

A BIG congratulations! You have made it through Chapter 2: Write The Vision, Make It Plain! I hope this has been helpful for you in developing and creating a business plan that makes sense for you and your practice.

＃ CHAPTER 3

Action Guide

The Business Plan

1. Mission Statement Prep:

   a) Define what you do.

   _____
   _____
   _____

   b) Intended target patient (who do you do for him or her?).

   _____
   _____
   _____
   _____

c) What makes your practice unique?

_____

_____

_____

_____

d) What problem are you solving (what value do you bring)?

_____

_____

_____

_____

2. Mission statement generation (4-5 sentences):

   a) Mission Statement

   _____

   _____

   _____

3. Business Description Statement Prep:

   a) What services are you offering?

   _____

   _____

   _____

b) How are these services unique?

c) Who will benefit from these services?

d) Why will they need it (what problem are you solving)?

e) Where will your practice be located?

f) How will you promote and market your practice?

g) What are your company goals?

4. Business Description (2-3 paragraphs):

5. Market Analysis

   a) Industry description and outlook:

   b) Target Market:

   c) Competitive analysis:

6. Start-up budget: (Great FREE resource!)

    a) http://www.entrepreneur.com/calculators/starting-costs.html

    ---

    ---

7. Financial Projections: (Great FREE resource!)

    a) https://www.score.org/resources/financial-projections-template

    ---

CHAPTER 4

Steps to a Strong Foundation

Last chapter, we focused on composing your business plan. In this chapter, we will focus our energy on developing a strong foundation for the setup of your medical practice.

DISCLAIMER: I am NOT a tax or legal consultant. You should consult with the appropriate professional(s) and complete your own research as it pertains to your state of residence before taking any definitive actions. I will provide you with general information; however, in an effort to get you started on reaching your goals. And with that, let's begin!

We will be covering the following topics in Chapter 3: corporation versus a sole proprietorship, business licensing, National Provider Identifier (NPI), obtaining a Tax Identifier Number (TIN) or Employer Identification Number (EIN) for your practice, bank accounts, accepting payments, malpractice insurance, other insurance coverage, and professional services.

Corporation Versus a Sole Proprietorship

There are several ways to setup your business. You can operate it as a sole proprietorship, set it up as a corporation, either as an S-Corp or C-Corp, or even operate it as a Limited Liability Company (commonly referred to as an "LLC"). Each business formation has its own benefits and drawbacks. As the solo practitioner of your own practice, it is vital that you setup your business in a way that will best serve your ultimate goals. To register your business as a corporation, you need to file certain documents, typically Articles of Incorporation, with your Secretary of State's offices. Contact your State Business Entity Registration Office to find out about specific filing requirements in the state where you plan on forming your business.

Sole proprietorship: This form of ownership ties the owner and the business together as one entity. As the owner, you are responsible for all of your practice's debts, but also enjoy all of its profits. The tax liability is yours for the entire amount of the net profits. A practice setup as a sole proprietorship is owned and run by one natural person. The owner has direct control, and is legally accountable for the practice's finances, including debts, loans, and losses. Although responsible for all of the practice's debts, the owner also has full control over the practice's assets. **Note:** A sole proprietorship means that a corporation has not been formed. Also, note that the terms sole or solo practitioner are not interchangeable with a sole proprietor.

S-Corporation: This form of corporation will enable all of the profits to be allocated to the practice's shareholders, so that the full earnings of the corporation are not a tax liability for you personally. Since you are one of the shareholders, possibly the controlling shareholder, you are only taxed on the amount you receive as an employee of your own corporation. In general, S-Corporations do not pay any federal income taxes. You are taxed on your earnings as an employee of the corporation, but earnings of the corporation itself are not taxed. Therefore, there is no double taxation.

Small businesses must meet certain eligibility requirements in order to become an S-Corporation in the United States. The small business cannot have more than one hundred shareholders; it cannot have an entity other than an individual person as a shareholder. In other words, another company or entity cannot be a shareholder. Further, the small business cannot have a non-resident as a shareholder, so all shareholders must be U.S. citizens. Finally, the small business cannot have more than one class of stock.

C-Corporation: Under the United States Federal Income Tax Law, a C-Corporation is an entity that is taxed separately from its owners. This means that the corporation itself, rather than the shareholders who own it, are held legally liable for the actions made and debts incurred on behalf of the corporation.

A C-Corporation is an independent legal entity, although a fictitiously created entity that has been created by law, which is owned by its shareholders. When the C-Corporation makes money, it pays corporate taxes on that money. Whatever is left over after taxes as retained earnings is either saved or spent. Retained earnings may also be distributed to the shareholders or stockholders as profits. As an employee of the corporation, your salary is also taxed at the normal rate of an individual person. Therefore, it's double taxation: the corporation is taxed on its earnings, and the salaries it pays out to its individual employees is also taxed. We usually see C-Corporation formations with many major companies.

A Limited Liability Company ("LLC"): Is a business that is structured similar to a sole proprietorship or general partnership. It is a business structure that combines the pass-through taxation of a partnership or sole proprietorship with the limited liability of a corporation. It is a pass-through entity, where all profits and losses pass through the business to the LLC owners, or members. According to the Internal Revenue Service ("IRS"), it is designed to provide the limited liability features of a corporation and the tax efficiencies and operational flexibility of a partnership. It is also important to know that an LLC is not a corporation. Similar to partnerships, the members themselves report the profits or losses on their individual federal tax returns, but not on the LLC's tax return. Nevertheless, some states do charge the LLC an income tax. Also, in certain states, like Texas, businesses that provide professional services that require a state professional license, such as legal or medical services, may not be allowed to form an LLC but may be required to form a very similar entity called a Professional Limited Liability Company ("PLLC"). My state of incorporation, Illinois, does not make such distinction, so it's important to research your state's policies and procedures for establishing an LLC.

Your job isn't over once your applications are in and your sole proprietorship, LLC, or corporation is formed. Even after formation, you must keep your business entity in compliance. If someone sues your practice and demonstrates that you have not maintained your LLC or corporation properly, your "corporation shield" can be pierced, making your personal assets vulnerable. This means you must keep your personal funds separate from those of the business and keep meticulous records. There can be no co-mingling of personal funds with corporate funds. Always use your business title when signing business documents so that it is beyond dispute that you were signing in your professional capacity. You also need to register your company's "Doing Business As" or "d/b/a" name. Just a side note about the d/b/a name, most corporations don't have to file fictitious names unless the corporations do business under names other than their own. So again, check with your individual state's county clerk office for more information on the rules and regulations. Other best business practices include sending in your annual statement or annual report at the time required by your state of incorporation, and keeping your address up to date so that you can refile your annual paperwork on time. If not, which I learned from personal experience, you will have to file additional paperwork and pay additional fees to reestablish your corporate status. In addition, you must file for a Foreign Qualification if you are operating in any state other than your state of incorporation. If you make any changes to your business, file an Articles of Amendment to make record of the change.

Business Licensing

A business license is a permit issued by a government agency that allows individuals or companies to conduct business within the government's geographical jurisdiction. It is the local government's authorization to start a business. Each of us has obtained a professional license as a physician in our respective states. In some states, this professional license is enough to establish a medical practice, and no further application for a separate business license is necessary. This is true for Illinois, where I practiced. Take note that business licenses vary between federal, state, and local government agencies

National Provider Identifier

National Provider Identifier ("NPI") is a unique identification number for covered healthcare providers, and each one of us has one. It was created to improve the efficiency and effectiveness of electronic transmission of health information. All healthcare providers who are HIPAA-covered entities, whether individually or as an organization, must obtain an NPI. The NPI will not change, even if your name, your address, or any other pertinent information changes. It does not carry certain information, like the state where you practice, your provider type, or your specialization.

There are two types of NPIs: Type 1 and Type 2. In a **Type 1 NPI**, if a physician is a sole proprietor, the physician may receive only one NPI, which would be the individual's NPI. The following factors do not affect whether the sole proprietor is an entity Type 1:

- The number of your practice's office locations;

- Whether your practice has employees; or

- Whether the IRS issued your practice an EIN so that your employees can use your EIN on their W2s, instead of your individual taxpayer identification number (which would be your social security number).

If you are a sole proprietor, you must apply for the NPI using your own social security number.

A **Type 2 NPI** is reserved for organizational healthcare providers. These providers are in a group. Do keep in mind that organizational healthcare providers may have a single employee or thousands of employees. For example, you started your corporation, but you are the only employee of your organization. You can have a separate NPI for your corporation, group practice, or organization. When you decide to expand your practice to include other physicians, they can practice under the group NPI. Note that if you expand your territory and add more locations, each location can operate under the same group NPI.

Taxes

Your **Tax Identification Number ("TIN")** or **Employer Identification Number ("EIN")** is what identifies you in your professional capacity to the government. The EIN, which is also known as a Federal Tax Identification Number, is used to identify a business entity. This is how you get paid by commercial insurance, and what you will use to set up your bank account and pay your taxes. You will need an EIN if you own or operate your business as a corporation or partnership, and/or if you have employees, including yourself. Otherwise, if you are operating as a sole proprietor, you will use your TIN, which is usually your social security number.

Banking

It's important to set up separate bank accounts for your practice's funds because you do not want to co-mingle funds from your personal account(s) with your business account(s). These are the things that you will need in order to setup your business bank account:

- Your certificate of incorporation, or if a sole proprietorship, your "Doing Business As" name;

- Your EIN number; and

- Funds for opening a balance (sometimes it only requires $25 to $100 to open up an account).

Again, from personal experience, I also recommend that you open a savings account and transfer a certain percentage of your income into the account regularly. This can be for an unexpected expense or to cover payroll, and will ensure that you continue to operate your practice in the black.

Merchant Accounts

A merchant account, or a point of sale device, will allow your business to accept credit card payments for the services it provides. These funds will be routed directly to your business bank account. Merchant accounts can be a little bit tricky. When starting out, I made the mistake of signing up with a merchant company that locked me in for about two years, and had a monthly fee of about $70. I setup the merchant account through my bank because it was offered when I setup my business account. I had been banking with them for seventeen years, and I knew nothing about merchant accounts, so I trusted they were going to serve the best interests of my practice. After completing my due diligence, I ended up using other merchants that had lower rates and processing fees without contracts. I had to pay a huge penalty for terminating the contract early. Money right down the drain! Lesson learned: Do your research. Some electronic health medical records offer merchant services directly through their systems for patients with easy payment options. I currently use an online bookkeeping agency, utilizing their end-to-end merchant, because it automatically records the transaction for tax purposes later, which makes my tax accountant very happy. There are also online merchants that do not require point of sale equipment. Instead, you will just need your laptop, iPad, or some other electronic system that accepts payment, and you will not be charged monthly fees.

Malpractice Insurance

We all need it, regardless of what medical field we practice in. Medical malpractice insurance protects you and your practice against claims of medical negligence. This insurance protects healthcare providers from litigious patients who allege claims that the physician was negligent or intentionally harmed them while receiving treatment. Your current employer likely already has medical malpractice insurance that covers your professional services, but physicians who open their own practices must purchase and pay for their own malpractice insurance policy. Even if you work as an independent contractor with other companies, you will still need to have your own malpractice insurance for the patients you see through your own private practice.

Insurance may be sold directly by an insurance company, by an agent representing your particular practice, or by an independent broker that sells the coverage packages of a number of companies. One advantage of buying insurance through an independent broker is that the broker offers the products of a number of companies. This ensures that you are able to shop around for the best deals. I recommend having multiple brokers at your service. I can recall when my insurance premium went up by $600 per month simply because my introductory rate had run out and not because of any negative marks against me, such as a patient bringing claims against my practice. Because the annual increase would have totaled $7,200.00 for the entire year, I asked my broker to find a better deal. Unfortunately, she was unable to do so. I decided to reach out to another broker who had a different group of insurance companies he was working with. He got a deal that saved my practice over $400 a month compared to the other broker's best offer. So again, you must do your due diligence in order to secure the best deal possible for your practice.

Other Types of Insurance to Consider

If you decide to continue to work full-time and pursue your private practice, it is best that you keep the health insurance benefits offered by your full-time employer. However, once you completely separate from your full-time employer, and begin to work on your private practice on a full-time basis, then you will need to purchase health insurance on your own. You will want to maintain a life insurance policy, obviously, to protect you and your family if something were to happen to you. You should also consider disability insurance. I never seriously considered disability insurance until I became sick and was out for an entire week. Because I was a solo practitioner, my business just completely shut down. My relatively minor illness caused me to think about what would happen if something more permanent were to affect my ability to work. What if I got into a car accident, and was never able to practice medicine again? What would I do then? Disability insurance is a good way to protect yourself in the event of a longer lasting illness, injury, or accident.

Other Potential Professional Services

You may want to consider a tax accountant to help you navigate your taxes as a business owner in an incorporated business. No one wants Uncle Sam looking for him or her. Also, consider having a financial advisor who can help you maximize your income, which includes actions like setting up a savings account or an investment account, such as 401Ks and IRAs, to prepare you for retirement. Additionally, an attorney can help you incorporate your business, prepare physician agreements, or draft other business contracts. I also recommend forming a relationship with a trusted mentor. This person should be someone who is experienced in maintaining a successful private practice, and who can keep you on track and help to avoid potential mistakes. It's preferable to have more than one trusted mentor to offer you multiple perspectives.

Remember to build your business from the inside out. The foundation that you build today is what will keep your business afloat in the future.

CHAPTER 4

Action Guide

Building a Strong Foundation

Check List

1. Name of business (or Doing Business As [DBA]):

   _____

2. Type of Business Entity

   ☐ Sole Proprietor

   ☐ S-Corporation

   ☐ C-Corporation

   ☐ Limited Liability Company (LLC)

   Other: _____

3. Business License (if required by your state)

4. Individual NPI

5. Group NPI (for clinic/group practice)

6. Employer Identification Number (EIN)/Tax Identification Number (TIN)

7. Business Bank Account

    ☐ Checking

    ☐ Savings

8. Merchant Account

9. Insurance

    ☐ Malpractice

    ☐ Health

    ☐ Life

    ☐ Disability

CHAPTER 5

How To Get Paid

Congratulations on making it to Chapter 5! You are now more than half way through the Lunchtime Physician Entrepreneur Blueprint! So, how's it going? Give yourself a high five for making it this far. Now, give yourself a pat on the back if you've been diligently working through your Action Guides. You rock! With all this preparation and foundation laying, your next question I'm sure is, "Now how do I get paid?" Having a solid understanding of the various payment models will be key to navigating your way to a successful and profitable practice. So, are you ready? Ok, let's go!

In this chapter we will dive into the intricacies of the insurance world, whether it be public, Medicare, Medicaid, or commercial insurance. We will also talk about the current healthcare climate with the Affordable Care Act, as well as discuss the option of having a cash-paying business or concierge service.

As residents and employed physicians, our main concerns were taking care for our patients, charting, ordering tests, and imaging. Because we have always been preoccupied with other tasks, most of us have never understood what was going on at the registration desk when our patients presented their insurance information. Our limited knowledge of insurance most likely stems from our experiences as patients ourselves, trying to decide between choosing an HMO or PPO from the plans our employer offered. As an entrepreneurial physician who plans to start his or her own practice, it is important to have, at a minimum, a general understanding of the insurance game and how it's played. Insurance, especially, affects how you will get reimbursed for the services that you provide.

Medicare and Medicare Advantage Plans

When you think about Medicare, what comes to mind? The elderly population? The Red, White, and Blue card? But what exactly is Medicare? Who does it cover? How is it paid for? Well, if you are currently working and you take a look at your paycheck stub, you will see that Uncle Sam has issued a Medicare tax that is taken out of your check each pay period. That money goes into a fund that you will receive disbursements from when you become qualified for Medicare, assuming the fund is still adequately funded. To be eligible, you must be age 65 or older and a U.S. citizen or permanent legal citizen for at least five years. The enrollee or their spouse must also have paid Medicare taxes for at least ten years. People under 65 who have received disability benefits for at least two years are also eligible, in addition to people of all ages with End-

Stage Renal Disease requiring dialysis or kidney transplant and people who have ALS.

Medicare covers an assortment of health care costs for the eligible individual. **Medicare Part A** helps cover inpatient care in hospitals, including critical access hospitals and skilled nursing facilities, but not custodial or long-term care. Most eligible individuals don't pay a premium for Medicare Part A because, as mentioned above, they or their spouses already paid for it through their payroll taxes when working. But the patient can, and will, incur some costs in the form of co-pays for hospital stays and skilled nursing facilities. Medicare also helps cover hospice care and some home healthcare. Hospice benefits are for terminally ill patients who have less than six months to live. Hospice benefits cover 100% of the patient's medical care, with the exception of medications, with no co-pay or deductible required by Medicare Part A.

If you have done any type of hospital work, you are familiar with the hospital trying to crack down on hospital readmissions. Not only do these readmissions contribute to poor patient outcomes, but the hospital itself loses money. If the hospital has an above average number of patients readmitted within thirty days of discharge, Medicare can actually take back the payments made on behalf of these patients, and the hospital can be subjected to an additional fine of 4 to18x the initial payment that was made. The readmission penalties apply to some of the most common causes of readmission:

pneumonia, heart failure, heart attacks, COPD, knee replacement, hip replacement.

Medicare Part B, on the other hand, covers outpatient physician and nursing services. It also covers ancillary services, including X-rays, laboratory and diagnostic tests, outpatient hospital procedures, and limited ambulance transportation. It also covers chemotherapy and immunosuppressive drugs; medical equipment, which includes canes, walkers, wheelchairs, and mobility scooters for those with mobility impairments; prosthetic devices, such artificial limbs or breast prosthesis following mastectomy; and it covers in-home oxygen.

So what does Medicare Part B cost? An enrollee pays a monthly payment, and depending on his or her income, that is usually taken directly out of the social security check, if requested. After the deductible is met, which is $147.00, then Medicare will cover 80% of approved medications and services. The remaining 20% is paid by the patient or by the secondary private insurance, which is also known as **Medi-Gap Insurance**.

Now let's talk about **Medicare Advantage** plans (or **"MA"** plans), often called **Medicare Part C** plans. These are health insurance programs of managed health care PPOs, which are Preferred Provider Organizations, or HMOs, which are Health Maintenance Organizations. They serve as substitutes for the original Medicare Parts A and B. Most MA Plans include the **Part D** prescription drug benefit plans, and are known as Medicare Advantage Prescription Drug Plans ("MAPDs"). The federal government makes separate payments to plans for providing Part D benefits. Original Medicare claims are processed through the Centers for Medicare and Medicaid Services (the "CMS"). In contrast, MA is offered by commercial insurance companies who received compensation from the government to provide all Part A and Part B benefits to enrollees, but do not process claims through the CMS.

Medicare pays "**Capitation**," which is a set amount every month for each member on the private health plan. On most Medicare Advantage plans, an enrollee must use in-network doctors or hospitals. For out-of-network providers, an enrollee may have to pay more or cover all expenses out-of-pocket. Most people pay the Part B premium of $104.90 each month, depending on their incomes, plus the monthly premium for the MA plan. In addition, the enrollee might pay a co-payment or co-insurance for covered services.

Once the out of pocket maximum is reached for an individual, the plan will pay 100% of services for the remainder of the calendar year with no lifetime maximum, so as long as the individual uses in-network providers. Persons who enroll in a Medicare Advantage HMO cannot use certain specialists or out of network providers without prior authorization from the HMO, except in emergencies. This will be a problem for those who need to use specialists, or who have been hospitalized and are forced to use out-of-network doctors while in the hospital. Enrolling in a PPO plan, if available, can help solve this dilemma because a PPO plan permits a subscriber to use any physician or hospital without prior authorization, but at a somewhat higher expense.

Enrollment in the MA plans has grown from 5.4 million in 2005, to a whopping 17.6 million in 2016, thanks to the Affordable Care Act. I can speak, however, to the frustration that some physicians have faced during this massive enrollment. For example, a patient may be assigned to a physician that she or he has never seen before. Under the new system, the patient may have lost his or her PCP, which he or she may have had for years, because that physician no longer accepted the insurance. On the provider side, we had to get on board and start getting credentialed with as many of these plans as possible, so that we could provide care for these patients. Initially, I was forced to turn down patients left and right. I was also losing patients because I had to wait to get credentialed with these new plans. Being credentialed with Medicare alone was no longer enough.

Medicaid, CHIP, and Medicaid Managed Care

Medicaid is a social healthcare program for low-income individuals and families with limited resources due to socioeconomic disparities. It is the largest source of funding for health-related services for the low-income population in the United States. Medicaid is jointly funded by federal and state governments, but is administered by the individual states. Each state currently has broad leeway to determine who is eligible.

The federal government has mandated that each state provide certain mandatory benefits to those who are eligible. These benefits include, but are not limited to, physician services, home health services, nurse/midwife services, family planning services, laboratory and X-rays services, and more.

There is a wide range of other medical and health-related services that are considered optional Medicaid benefits, and the federal government does not mandate that a state provide these additional services.

The main criteria for Medicaid eligibility are limited income and financial resources, which plays no role in determining Medicare coverage. Medicare, in contrast, is mostly dependent upon age and disability rating. Medicaid also covers a wider range of healthcare services than Medicare. Some people are actually eligible for both Medicaid and Medicare, and are known as dual eligible. In 2001, about 6.5 million American were enrolled in both Medicare and Medicaid. In 2015 approximately 11 million qualified for Medicare and Medicaid.

Children's Health Insurance Plan (or "**CHIP**"): A child may be eligible for Medicaid, regardless of the eligibility status of his or her parents. Thus, a child may be covered by Medicaid based on his individual status even if his parents aren't eligible. Similarly, if a child lives with someone other than a parent, he may still be eligible based on his individual status. CHIP benefits are different in each state, but all states provide comprehensive coverage, including routine check-ups, immunizations, doctor visits, prescriptions, dental and vision care, inpatient and outpatient hospital care, laboratory and X-ray services, and emergency services.

Routine "well child" doctor and dental visits are free of charge, but there may be co-payments for other services. Some states charge a monthly premium for CHIP coverage. The costs are different in each state, but usually amount to no more than 5% of the family's income for the year.

Medicaid-Managed Care: This is an arrangement between a state Medicaid agency and a Managed Care Organization (or "MCO") that accepts a set payment or capitation for services. As of 2016, twenty-eight states had contracts with MCOs. There are a variety of different types of health plans that serve Medicaid-managed healthcare programs, including for-profit and non-profit Medicaid-focused and commercial plans, and independent community health center-owned programs. There are two main forms, Risk-Based MCO or Primary Care Case Management ("PCCM"). There is also a limited benefits plan. States can make managed care enrollment voluntary, or seek a waiver from CMS to require certain populations to enroll in an MCO. If a state can provide a choice between at least two plans, then they can make enrollment in an MCO mandatory.

Primary Care Case Management (or "PCCM"): This is where a primary care provider is responsible for proving and monitoring the care of the enrolled Medicaid beneficiaries. Typically, these providers are paid a small monthly case management fee, usually about three to four dollars, in addition to fee-for-service reimbursement for treatment.

Risk-Based Managed Care Organizations are the most common type of Medicaid-managed care arrangement. Each MCO is a group of doctors, clinics, hospitals, pharmacies, and other health care providers. It operates on a model similar to an HMO. Each Medicaid recipient chooses an MCO based on its location and the services it offers. The enrollee also choses a primary care physician, who will be coordinating his or her care. Once the selection is made, the enrollee cannot go outside of this network of providers, except for medical emergencies. In return, the MCO receives a fixed monthly fee to cover the enrollee, which is paid by the state where the enrollee resides. Now, here is where it gets interesting. If aggregate expenditures exceed total income, the MCO is responsible for absorbing the losses. Although, sometimes the health plan passes on a portion of the financial risk to the participating providers. How does this affect you as a provider? You won't receive reimbursement for a portion, or even all, of the services you provided. In addition, some states agree to share the financial risk with the health plan by assuming losses in excess of a specified level. A typical threshold, for example, is 107% of the aggregate payments. Such arrangements are often referred to as "Risk Corridors."

Commercial Insurance

Commercial Health Insurance plans are considered managed care plans as well. These commercial insurers have contracts with health care providers and medical facilities to provide care for members at reduced costs. These providers make up the plan's network. The natural question that follows is, "How much of your care will the plan pay for?" The answer depends on the network's rules. Plans that restrict your choices will usually cost less. If you want a flexible plan, it will probably be more expensive.

There are three types of managed care plans, and you have probably heard of all of them. They are **HMO, PPO, and Point of Service ("POS")**. An HMO plan usually only pays for care within the network. You will select a primary care doctor who is responsible for coordinating most of your care. A PPO plan will usually cover more costs, if you get care within the network. Nevertheless, the plan will still pay part of the resulting costs if you go outside of the network. POS plans let you choose between an HMO or PPO plan each time you need care. These plans may be provided by the employer or purchased by an individual, a family, or a small business.

Affordable Care Act

Since the passage of the Affordable Care Act ("ACA") on March 23, 2010, and signed by former President Barack Obama, about 16.4 million uninsured people have gained health coverage. Those gains are primarily attributable to the marketplace, young adults who have stayed on their parents' plans after turning 26 years old, and Medicaid expansions.

Some of the benefits of the ACA include an expansion of Medicaid to cover more low-income Americans. The ACA increased Medicaid eligibility limits to 133% of the federal poverty level by covering adults without dependents. The ACA also provides free preventative healthcare exams, and a subsidy to low- and middle-income Americans to help buy insurance. Lastly, it provides a central health insurance exchange or marketplace where the public can compare policies and rates.

The Health Insurance Exchanges: The Affordable Health Care Act established state-based insurance exchanges. These exchanges are regulated online marketplaces, administered either by federal or state governments, where individual or small businesses can purchase private insurance plans. Only approved plans that meet service standards can be sold on the exchanges, and insurers can no longer deny applicants on the basis of a pre-existing condition. Consumers can visit these online marketplaces, compare the plans that they offer, fill out the necessary forms, and have their eligibility determined.

The final step is to purchase the chosen insurance plan during the limited open enrollment periods.

Concierge Medicine

On a completely separate note from insurance, Concierge Medicine is a term used to describe the relationship between a patient and a primary care physician where the patient pays the physician directly through a retainer. In exchange, the PCP provides enhanced care, which usually includes a limited patient load for the provider to ensure adequate time and availability for each patient. Concierge Medicine may also be referred to as retainer medicine, membership medicine, cash only practice, or direct care. This type of service, regardless of what it is called, is a paid model that allows the physician to collect annual payments for the services he or she rendered.

There are three types of Concierge Medicine: (1) fee for care, (2) fee for extra care, and (3) a hybrid between the two.

1. **The Fee For Care ("FFC")** is an annual retainer model where the patient pays a monthly, quarterly, or annual retainer fee to the physician. The retainer fee covers most services provided by the physician in his or her office. Oftentimes, services such as vaccinations, lab work, X-rays, and other similar services are excluded, and charged for separately on a cash basis. Some offices will only accept direct payments, rather than insurance coverage, al-

though they often encourage patients to have insurance to cover unexpected hospital stays and emergency room care.

2. **The Fee For Extra Care ("FFEC")** is similar to the FFC model. The main difference is that additional services not covered by the plan are charged to Medicare or the patient's insurance plan. Some of the benefits and services typically included in the FFC or FFEC retainer models are same-day access, immediate cell phone and text messages, cell phone, text messages, and online consultation, unlimited office visits with no co-pay, little or no waiting time in the office, convenient appointment scheduling, an emphasis on preventative care, an unhurried atmosphere, and prescription refills. Many FFC and FFEC retainer plans can be purchased with pre-taxed dollars, utilizing HSA or FSA accounts, which are available through the patient's insurance plans.

3. **A Hybrid Concierge Model** enables physicians to charge a monthly, quarterly, or annual retainer or membership fee for services that Medicare and insurers do not cover, but they can also see patients with commercial and/or public insurance. The extra services provided under a hybrid model may include email access, phone consultations, newsletters, extended visits, comprehensive wellness and evaluation plans, and telemedicine consultations. For all covered services under this type of plan,

the bills will be sent and covered by Medicare and/or the insurance company. This model allows the physician to continue to see their non-retainer patients, while also providing their concierge patients increased or special service for an additional fee.

Ancillary Services

Depending on your specialty or budget, you can add ancillary services to your practice to help generate income. You can either bill an insurance or charge a fee to be paid directly by the patient. Some of these services include, but of course, are not limited to, imaging, X-rays and ultrasounds, diagnostic testing, EKG, phlebotomy, Holter monitoring, and laboratory work. You can actually have your own lab, but you must have Clinical Laboratory Improvement Amendments (CLIA) certifications and waivers. Other services include dermatologic procedures, including Botox, laser, mole removal, and fillers; procedures such as casting, splinting, and steroid injections. Telemedicine, where a provider speaks to a patient via their mobile device, is rapidly becoming a popular stream of income for practices as it addresses urgent/acute care without the patient coming into the office. You may also want to consider hiring other licensed professionals who carry their own malpractice insurance and business licenses as independent contractors to provide services if you are considering going the medspa route. These professionals include but are not limited to massage therapists, estheticians, naturopaths, and acupuncturists.

When building a successful practice, there is no straight line to financial success. If you are trying to figure out which payment model is best for your practice, know that a single model is probably not the solution. It's important to diversify your portfolio of payers, just like you would investments, so that you can maintain a steady stream of income. Now that you are equipped with the basic knowledge of these payer models, it's time to get creative and be innovative in seeking out potential revenue streams for your practice.

CHAPTER 5

Action Guide

How To Get Paid

Design what your "Payer Portfolio" will look like.

1. Use the resources to research which insurance providers (public and commercial) are relevant in your state, and decide which plans you will apply for.

2. Are you considering a Concierge Model? Which one?

3. Are you going to provide any ancillary or additional services?

CHAPTER 6

Practice Management

In this chapter, we will be discussing the ins and outs of the medical billing process, which is something that most physicians, including myself prior to starting my own practice, have very little knowledge about. We will also cover hospital credentialing, and all the perks that go along with it. Specifically, we will discuss medical billing, the billing process, diagnostic and procedure coding, electronic health records, billing services, and hospital credentialing. We will also touch on hospital privileges and contract work. Are you ready to get started? Let's dive in!

Medical Billing

The medical practice's financial health relies heavily on the billing office. In order to support the decrease in reimbursement by payers and increased demands on the providers, it's vital to have highly skilled individuals running the billing office to optimize the practice's revenue performance. A medical biller must be equipped with the knowledge and understanding of medical insurance, the claims process, the appeals process, and the impact each has on the practices revenue.

The Billing Process: The billing cycle, also referred to as the revenue cycle, is the interaction between a healthcare provider and the insurance company or other payer. This cycle can take days or months to complete, and oftentimes requires multiple cycles before resolution of the bill is complete. The billing cycle begins with the office visit, and ends with reimbursement for the services rendered. In my opinion, it is vital for both the physician, as well as the medical biller, to be comfortable with medical and procedure coding. This knowledge has the potential to reduce the time to reimbursement.

Unless you are just starting out with your own practice, the medical billing process typically involves multiple individuals. As a solo practitioner, you may wear many hats, including medical billing and coding. Medical coding involves the front office administrators, such as the receptionist, as well as back office staff, including the medical biller and coder, if you're able to hire them. The process begins with the patient check in. First, a patient calls to setup an appointment. If it is a patient's first visit, necessary information is collected by the office staff or physician to prepare for the patient visit. Patient demographical information includes the name, address, and phone number, and is collected for the medical record. Insurance information is also collected, including the name of the insurance provider and the policy and group number.

I have found it to be quite helpful to obtain insurance information prior to the scheduled appointment, in order to make a determination of whether the practice accepts the patient's insurance plan. Obtaining billing information prior to the appointment saves you and the patient time.

After the doctor sees the patient, the diagnosis and procedure codes are assigned. These codes assist the insurance company in determining coverage and whether the medical services provided were necessary.

ICD-10: Before we move on through the billing cycle, let's pause and talk a little bit about what coding is and how it affects reimbursement. We are all familiar with the ICD system because we enter diagnostic codes daily. But what is ICD? ICD is the acronym for the International Statistical Classification of Diseases and Related Health Problems, or for short, the International Classification of Diseases, which is maintained by the World Health Organization ("WHO"). This system is designed to classify a wide variety of signs, symptoms, abnormal findings, complaints, social circumstances, and external causes of injury or disease by assigning them designated codes. As of October 1, 2015, we moved on to ICD-10, which is a more detailed classification.

ICD-10 consists of two parts. Part one, ICD-10-CM, is diagnostic coding, which is used in all U.S. healthcare settings. Part two, ICD-10-PCS, is inpatient procedure coding, which is used for all U.S. hospital settings. ICD-10 affects diagnosis and inpatient procedure coding for everyone covered by HIPAA, not just those who submit Medicare/Medicaid claims. The change to ICD-10 does not affect CPT coding for outpatient procedures.

CPT codes stands for the Current Procedural Terminology, Fourth Edition. For more than four decades, physicians and other healthcare professionals have relied on CPT to communicate with colleagues, patients, hospitals, and insurers about the procedures they have performed. CPT is a listing of descriptive terms and identification codes that are used for reporting medical, surgical, and diagnostic services. Each code has a specific five-digit number and description, as well as a reimbursable value. This information is used for claims processing and developing guidelines for medical care review.

Before a patient's bill can be officially recorded and sent off to the payer, it first must satisfy certain official requirements. One of the biggest hurdles to clear is that the bill must be compliant with HIPAA requirements and the office of the Inspector General.

After the physician or medical coder has translated the patient's diagnosis and treatments into the universal language of ICD and CPT coding, the medical bill can be created. The medical biller will then transmit this claim to the insurance company.

A bill is usually transmitted electronically by formatting the claim and using the electronic data interchange to submit the claim file to the payer directly or via a clearinghouse. This method is the most efficient and accurate way to process claims, and it saves the healthcare industry and your practice a significant amount of money compared to paper submissions. In fact, one of the reasons that the ICD system migrated from ICD-9-CM to ICD-10 is because the newer code is more flexible and optimized for electronic usage. Submitting claims electronically reduces the amount of manual data the medical biller must input, thereby reducing the amount of errors made, and subsequently, increasing the amount of clean claims submitted to health insurers. Following a submission, the payer will respond by acknowledging that the claim submission was received, and that it was accepted for further processing. When the claim or claims are actually processed by the payer, the payer will ultimately respond in the form of **explanation of benefits ("EOBs")** or **electronic remittance advice ("ERAs")**, which will have the line items of the claim that will be paid or denied. If denied, the response will provide the reason for why it was denied. The physician or medical biller can then make corrections to the bill, resubmit it, and the process starts all over again. This exchange of claims and denials may be repeated multiple times until a claim is paid in full, or until the provider relents and accepts an incomplete reimbursement.

Clearing Houses: Remember, you can either submit a claim directly to the payer, or submit through a clearing house. A clearing house is a third-party operation that acts as a middleman between the healthcare providers and the insurance carriers. They are able to "scrub" the claims clean of errors. They format the claims correctly, in accordance with HIPAA and insurance standards. Clearing houses forward the claims to the appropriate parties. Typically, clearing houses use internal software to receive claims from healthcare providers. A third-party clearing house is necessary because healthcare providers typically have to send a high volume of insurance claims each day to many different insurance providers. To complicate the process, each of these insurance providers may have their own submission standards. Using a clearing house to submit claims will decrease the potential for mechanical error by the medical biller, and will also decrease the time required for formatting each claim to each specific insurance carrier.

Receiving Payments: When a provider agrees to accept the insurance company's plan, the plan's contractual agreement includes fee schedules, which dictate what the insurance company will pay the provider for covered procedures. The plan's contract will also dictate timeliness of filings. We, as providers, typically submit charges that are more for services, rather than what has been negotiated by the physician and the insurance company. This is documented on what we call a superbill. Because each insurance plan may pay a different percentage of the amount billed, we submit a fee that is higher to cover this discrepancy. As a result, the expected payment from the insurance company for services is lower than the submitted amount based on what agreement you have with the insurance company. The amount that is paid by the insurance company is known as the allowable amount. The insurance payment is further reduced if the patient has a co-pay (which is paid directly to the provider by the patient), a deductible that has to be met, or co-insurance that will cover the remaining balance of the patient's bill.

Collecting Payments: When a patient has been sent a bill with the remaining balance for the medical services provided, a payment date is set and listed on the bill itself. You have experienced this process yourself when you go to the doctor and receive a bill for the services that were rendered. Once the patient's payment is received, and the healthcare provider has been reimbursed for all services provided (co-pay, insurance reimbursement, patient's balance), the information is filed in the patient's record, and the transaction is effectively closed. If the patient fails to pay a bill on time, the healthcare provider is responsible for following-up with the patient and handling any billing issues. If the balance remains unpaid for a certain amount of time, the physician can institute a collection process in order to be reimbursed for the overdue bill. The physician's financial policy determines the amount of time allotted before the collection process (usually through a third party collection agency for a fee) is instated, and how to go about collecting the reimbursement. I recommend that you have the patient sign a document stating that he or she is aware of your financial policy prior to receiving your medical services

Let's just do a quick recap of the billing cycle:

- The patient schedules an appointment.

- All insurance information is collected prior to the visit to determine if the practice accepts the insurance.

- The patient comes into your office for initial or subsequent visits.

- He or she checks in, providing all of the pertinent demographical and physical proof of insurance (insurance cared) to be entered into the electronic medical record.

- The patient is then seen and treated by physician/provider.

- At the end of the patient's visit, a superbill is created, whereby the physician or medical coder enters diagnostic codes (ICD-10) and procedure codes (CPT) in addition to the amount billed for those services.

- The bill then goes to your medical biller, which is either in-house or outsourced, and the biller sends the claim to the insurance company or to the clearing house.

- The insurance company accepts the claim and generates an EOB or ERA, stating whether the medical claim has been accepted or denied.

- If accepted, the insurance company remits payment (if not, the claim gets resubmitted after making the necessary adjustments to improve the likelihood of payment until the insurance company remits payment).

- Any remaining balance on the bill is the responsibility of the patient. If the patient pays the remaining balance, the billing cycle is closed. If it is not, a collection process ensues to receive reimbursement for the services rendered.

Medical Billing Services

Once your practice grows and reaches it ability to handle all of its own paperwork, most medical providers will look to outsource their medical billing process to a third-party known as a medical billing service. These billing services typically take a percentage of the practice's revenue as payment. Another option is to hire an internal medical biller who works solely on your practice's medical claims, who would be salaried or paid hourly. Do what makes the most financial sense for your business, but either way, it lightens your load as a sole practitioner. Many of these medical billing service providers offer electronic health records ("EHR") or electronic medical records ("EMR") to help increase customer satisfaction and optimize the provider's workflow.

Electronic Health Record ("EHR"): Is basically the digital version of a patient's medical chart. It provides you information in real-time, and it makes information available instantly and securely to authorized users. You can also securely share information with your patients via patient portals, as well as with other clinicians. You can prescribe more reliably through E-prescribing, which is the electronic submission of prescriptions. You are also able to send and receive orders, reports, and patient results digitally. This system can also be setup to warn or send reminders about patient care. In addition, you are able to submit claims electronically for reimbursement. Personally, I really enjoyed being a paperless clinic, and did not miss the huge filing cabinets that could have potentially taken up floor space in my office.

Not only is EHR convenient and efficient, it is now mandated. Federal and state governments, insurance companies, and other large medical institutions are heavily promoting the adoption of EMRs. EMRs and EHRs are used interchangeably. The United States Congress has devised a formula of incentives and penalties for EMR adoption versus continued use of paper records as part of the Health Information Technology for Economic and Clinical Health ("HITECH Act"). If you're considering accepting Medicare and Medicaid patients, then you should definitely consider using an EMR.

Credentialing

Let's talk about credentialing at hospitals, and how it may benefit your practice. Hospitals grant privileges to physicians, which come in different categories, including admitting privileges, courtesy privileges, and surgical privileges. Admitting privileges allow the physician to admit a patient to the hospital. Courtesy privileges allow the physician to occasionally admit, visit, and treat patients in the hospital. Surgical privileges allow the physician surgeon to perform surgery in the hospital's operating room or outpatient surgery facilities. Each hospital has its own set of rules, regulations, and policies regarding how a physician can admit and treat patients. Usually, the hospital requires the physician to submit a written application to obtain his or her privileges. The application contains extensive information about the physician's education, licensing, and experience. The hospital's credentialing committee then decides whether to grant these privileges to the physician. The committee thoroughly reviews the physician's application, and usually conducts an in-person interview, before voting to accept or deny the physician's application. There is almost always a fee associated with submitting one of these applications, so choose your hospitals wisely, preferably in the vicinity of your practice.

I find several advantages to hospital credentialing. If you admit your patients into a hospital, you are able to bill insurance companies for treating your patients in this setting, as well as foster continuity of care for the patient. Credentialing also allows physicians in surgical specialties to accept surgical cases, and again, they can bill for these services. Additionally, some hospitals either outsource their pooled physicians, or directly hire physicians who can take emergency room or hospital shifts (i.e. hospitalists). The hospital will usually cover your malpractice insurance while you're conducting these shifts at their facilities, which is great for internal medicine, pediatric physicians, psychiatrists, obstetricians, or family medicine doctors. These additional hospital shifts and billable services are also great sources of additional income as you continue to grow your practice. Make sure, however, that your contract specifies whether you are operating as an independent contractor or as an employee, as each has its own tax and legal implications. Consult your lawyer and tax accountant to determine what type of contract will benefit your practice most.

While building your own private medical practice, you will find yourself wearing many hats. You job description will have enlarged overnight, and you are now responsible for more than just patient care. You are now also in charge of the management of your practice, and the tasks that were once completed by the magical worker bees at your former employer, will now need to be covered by you. When you are first starting out, you will likely handle every magical worker bee task. Accordingly, it's important that you learn about, understand, and actually execute, initially, all of the moving parts in order to be successful. As your business grows, then you will be able to outsource what you choose not to handle directly. The takeaway is that you will never know what the issue is, let alone how to fix it, if you never took the time to learn the process in the first place.

CHAPTER 7

Invest in Yourself

Woo-hoo! You made it to the end! I pray this blueprint has been helpful to you, and has shed some light on some of the processes that are necessary to consider before opening your own private medical practice. Our final chapter will focus on investing in yourself because no one else will, until they see you have some skin in the game. In this chapter, we'll talk about spiritual health, physical health, mental health, professional development, having an accountability partner, financial health, capital building, and why it's important to invest in your community. So what are we waiting for? Let's get to it! Well it's personal testimony time, again. When I decided to go into private practice, it was more of a passion move, rather than a business move. I did not like how my colleagues and I were being treated by the administrators at our FQHC employer. The pay was low, and the hours were long and arduous. I typically worked from 8 p.m. to 5 p.m. every day. Perhaps my biggest grievance was that by the time our FQHC patients finally reached my office, they were usually very disgruntled and I had very little time to spend with them, which would often compound their frustration. Moreover, the bonuses and incentives that were intended for the physician never reached the intended source. They were allegedly "regenerated" back into the FQHC. Needless to say, morale was low, the physician turnaround was high, and I was extremely unhappy.

The position at the FQHC was my first job as a physician. I was fresh out of residency, and I felt like I was becoming jaded with the medical profession way too early in my career. I figured that there must be a better way to work in this field and practice the medicine I loved. From the moment I first realized that what I was making for the FQHC in one day was what they were paying me every two weeks, I completely lost all desire to work for someone else! I had no idea what I was jumping into, or how to go about doing it, but I knew I wanted to be my own boss. To complicate matters, I was not financially stable at the time of my professional epiphany. I had no nest egg or a" rainy day" fund to finance my career shift. I was basically living paycheck-to-paycheck. Although I lacked financial riches (heck, financial stability), I had, and still have to this day, an abundant faith in God, and I believed in the vision He gave to me. Plan A didn't work out for me, and I decided it was time to move on to Plan B.

The advice I am about to give is the kind of advice you might expect to receive from someone who really had to grind. Being an entrepreneur is a steep learning curve. You have to know and understand all aspects of your business, especially the finances. How you handle your personal finances is how you will handle your business finances. Be sure to handle all of your funds properly, and I highly recommend you have a financial advisor in your corner. Having a healthy bottom line and the proper financial advisors will take some sacrifice and frugality, but if you're serious about starting your medical practice, you will be able to make this happen.

This particular lesson is one of the many I learned during my struggle to open my practice. I, like many of you, was not born with the proverbial silver spoon in my mouth. I do not come from a wealthy family, and the money for my practice was not passed down to me. Moreover, investors were not lined up at my door to finance my vision. I also haven't always acted in the best interest of my financial future. Nevertheless, I have not let any of this adversity stop me. I can proudly say that during the three years I operated my private practice, it was debt-free from bank loans and I owned one hundred percent of my business without the assistance of investors. And when I am ready to do it all over again, I have the knowledge and expertise required to make the next practice just as, if not even more, successful. These are the same tools that I am imparting to you. I am a living, breathing example that you too can start your own medical practice, but you have to find the courage to invest in yourself.

Spiritual Health

Ultimately, we have no control over the consequences of our actions. We can do our very best, and put forth our best efforts, but honestly, if it's not God's will, then what we seek will not be accomplished. I have found that by surrendering to God, it has allowed Him to work miracles in my life. Make your desires known to Him. Then do your part by preparing to achieve those desires, without attaching yourself to the outcome. The last step is the hardest one to do: let it go and give your aspirations and fears to Him. You will be surprised at what He will do in your life. It is this act of surrender that allows you to take the necessary leap of faith into the unknown. "Faith is the substance of things hoped for; the evidence of things not seen" (Hebrews 11:1.) You must trust that when you take this leap of faith, peace will come when you either land gently, or learn that you can fly. Spiritual growth is essential to entrepreneurship because there will be many ups and downs in your business. Arming yourself with God's promises will equip you to handle whatever may come your way. Know that it is all working out for your good! This is good news!

Physical Health

Now, as a physician, I'm going to give you a dose of your own medicine. It is time for you to truly invest in your physical health. How many times a day do we emphasize to our patients how important exercise and eating a proper diet are for maintaining a healthy lifestyle? If we are honest with ourselves, how often are we actually putting our own advice into practice? As you can imagine, starting a new business can be stressful, and we, especially, are acutely aware of how stress can wreak havoc on the body. Make it your priority to get in the habit of exercising at least three to five times a week, preferably the latter. Be sure that your daily diet is infused with ample servings of fruits and vegetables and devoid of unhealthy fats, cholesterol, and simple sugars. As we know, these actions have many benefits beyond merely looking good. You are more productive, your mind is sharper, your mood is improved, and you have more energy. As you build your business in your spare time, you will be adding more responsibility to your plate. Wouldn't the benefits of exercise and a healthy diet be the boost you need? Stamina is absolutely the key to entrepreneurship, so train for the game. Invest in your physical health.

Mental Health

You also have to invest in your mental health. I love the verse Proverbs 23:7 that says, "As a man thinketh, in his heart so he is." Positive affirmations are always a great way to stay motivated, and to keep your momentum moving forward. If you habitually tell yourself that you are capable of achieving great things, you will never stop striving to get better. Dream big, set audacious goals, and believe that you can accomplish them. The mind is a powerful tool. The moment you start saying

"I can't," you'll be right, and you won't. Invest in your mental health, and start thinking healthier, more positive thoughts.

Professional Development

Take the time to invest in professional development. There are many aspects of private practice, and running a business, in general, that are not innate. To be sure, the needed skills were not taught in medical school or residency. Understanding how a business works, and all of the intricacies of the process, is something that you will have to learn. You may decide to take the time and resources to go to business school if you so desire an M.B.A. Even if you choose not to attend school formally, trust and believe that you need to invest in workshops and/or courses to obtain the knowledge you don't possess. I took advantage of every online course, boot camp, and entrepreneurial workshop I could find to enhance my knowledge. All I knew was medicine, but I needed a much broader skill set. I had to learn about marketing, developing a business plan, revenue generation, and many other topics. I didn't just wake up with the knowledge and experiences to be successful. I had to invest in my professional development. Just like the field of medicine, professional development is a continual process. You must continually seek ways to grow your business, to take it to the next level. But let me just say, you deserve a big pat on the back for navigating through the blueprints of this book. You have officially started investing in your professional development. Kudos to you, and high-five! "Learning is a treasure that will follow its owner everywhere" ~ Chinese Proverb.

Accountability Partner

"Iron sharpens iron." Proverbs 27:17 is one of my favorite scriptures because it speaks to the people you decide to surround yourself with. Find yourself an accountability partner. Studies have shown that when someone else holds us accountable for our actions, we are most likely to follow through with them. If left to our own devices, we will give excuses, rationalize every bad decision, and procrastinate. By electing to have an accountability partner, you will be more likely to see progress. But remember, accountability is a two-way street. Take the time to invest in your accountability partner. Hold him or her accountable to the big dreams and lofty goals he or she is trying to achieve. Push each other, motivate each other, celebrate one another's wins, and help soften the blow of the losses. An accountability partner will prevent you from becoming self-consumed in your own process. The top can truly be a lonely place without someone to share it with.

Financial Health

Invest in your financial health. What are your financial goals? What do you need to do to get there? Among our peers in the profession, money is seriously a taboo topic. Most of us are earning more money than the average American, even us primary care physicians, but are we accumulating wealth? Are we preparing ourselves for retirement? Are we increasing our net worth? Are we investing and saving? Can we pass down generational wealth? Or are we spending more than we are bringing in? Ask yourself, are you living above your means? Are you living paycheck-to-paycheck? Place your fingers on your financial pulse? Is it on its way to financial arrest? Now is the time to start thinking and preparing for your financial future, if you have not done so already. Starting your own business is definitely not a get-rich-quick scheme. It takes some financial know-how to get it going and keep it going. How you manage your personal money will reflect how you will manage your business's money. I can't emphasize that point enough. Therefore, it's essential to develop and/or optimize good financial habits now. Obtaining a financial planner is one way to begin this journey.

If I can, I'd like to briefly talk about tithing. Tithing is giving God the first tenth of your income, and it signifies your faith that God can provide for all of your needs. I first began tithing in 2009, and have not stopped since. As I look back over my life, I realize that God has neither failed me, nor has He left me to fend for myself. As I shared with you in Chapter One, my mom developed dementia at an early age. I was a first-year resident taking care of my mom on a fifty-thousand-dollar a year residency income. The cost of caretakers alone would wipe me out financially. I made the decision to start tithing, and literally, God started making a way for me. When I was down to my last dollar, I would mysteriously come into some large sum of money that would last me through the next crisis. Even when I struck out on my own, divine opportunities seemed to present themselves around every corner, so I named my business **Divine** Aesthetics Medspa & Wellness Center. I knew where my help came from. Even when I thought my business would go under, some way, somehow, all of my bills were paid. I did not always have a fancy car or a big house, but I've always been provided with what I needed. There has always been food in the refrigerator, clothes on our backs, and a roof over our heads. Having faith is more than simply believing, it's putting your life in God's hands, and asking that He do His will to build His Kingdom. This is, and always will be, a part of my financial plan. For every dollar I earn, I give back God His ten cents. Your thing may not be tithing, but I encourage you to become an avid giver to those less fortunate, and to those whose ministry and mission is to serve the disadvantaged. Your blessings will come!

Invest in Yourself

So how much money do you really need to start a business? When you think of starting a business, the first thing that usually comes to mind is, "Where the heck am I going to get the money to pay for this?" Then the questions start to flow, "Where do I even start? Do I take my business plan and go to the bank and ask for a loan? Do I ask my family and friends to help out? Do I resort to social media and start a crowdfunding campaign? Do I have a mass garage sale, and just start getting rid of stuff?" So many questions, so many questions.

Your timeline for when you would like to start your business will determine how aggressive you will be in building capital for your venture. I only gave myself three months from the time I put in my letter of resignation at the FQHC to my last day as an employee. I was on a more accelerated course. In retrospect, I didn't give myself enough time to build as much capital as I would have liked or needed. I left my job in August, and by October, I had opened the doors to my clinic. I was not as ready as I could have been, which is the reason I wrote this book. I want to provide you with the blueprint to optimize your success rate. So what do you think? Let's talk about building some financial capital.

The Action Guide after this chapter focuses on determining your startup costs. These may vary depending on your medical specialty. Once you compile a realistic budget, it's time to grind and stick to it.

I want to give you an opportunity to think outside the box. Do you remember when you were looking for a job after residency? Did you use physician recruiters and post your job resume on career sites to explore as many options as possible? Was your e-mail inbox flooded with opportunities? Well, I never took my name or my résumé off any of those sites. To this day, I continue to receive emails from physician recruiters constantly telling me about the next opportunity. I use this information to my advantage. When I am low on cash, or my business is experiencing a lull, I use these recruiters to generate more income. I then take what I learn from the temporary position, and try to incorporate the knowledge and experience into my practice to increase my revenue.

I'm going to tell you a little bit about some of the part-time or moonlighting positions that I have had. When I was in residency my third-year, after taking my boards, I received my professional license. Many don't know it, but that gives you the right to actually practice as an attending physician while in residency. So I first sought out a part-time position that could supplement my residency income. I found a company that specialized in doing home visits to patients who were homebound and unable to make it to the doctor's office. I started with them, working after my half days and clinic and on the weekends. I literally doubled my income in my last year of residency just by doing this. Not only that, but when I started my practice during those three months of planning, while still employed by the FQHC, I started to build my own contingent of patients that were elderly or disabled to do home visits to them. I did not have a brick-and-mortar building yet, but I was building my practice through these early provider–patient relationships. I would do a full day of work, then go see a couple of patients in their homes before I was done for the day. I would then use my Saturdays to see the remaining patients. I have used what I learned from moonlighting in residency, and incorporated it into my own private practice, building capital that went toward my brick and mortar office. Are you guys getting it?

I also try to find flexible part-time positions that I can do simultaneously with other tasks. For instance, I found a telemedicine company that was looking for a physician PRN. The position had only a few requirements: (1) a specific state license and (2) a computer with Wi-Fi and webcam capabilities. I chose evening hours that worked with my schedule, when I would be at home winding down or taking care of my mother. I would also make time during the day, between answering calls and patient visits

This flexible, part-time position has recently turned into something much bigger. I have ended up taking on a full-time position with this company. They have licensed me in 15 states, including California, which is where I have recently moved to with my husband to follow his ministry as pastor of a church in Sacramento, after closing my practice. See how God orchestrated my steps? I now work from home, full-time, while I pursue other entrepreneurial endeavors. I am currently planning to open a medical clinic for the disadvantaged in Sacramento, California, with my husband as he has a passion for serving the homeless and disadvantaged through his ministry. Always keep the doors open so that when opportunity knocks, you are not only there to answer, but you can continue to create your own opportunities!

I love part-time and moonlighting positions because they don't typically require a long-term commitment. They present an opportunity for financial growth in your spare time, and you gain new experiences that you can then incorporate into your own practice. You also earn additional income, which reduces financial pressure. A win-win-win right? Best of all, opportunities abound. As your practice grows, you can scale down on these part-time positions to meet the demands of your business. Alternatively, when things are slow, you can increase your hours or find new experiences to explore. The ultimate goal is to increase your earning potential for saving or investing, so that you don't have to take out a loan or sell ownership rights to your business. Your hustle and grind pays off!

Here is a list of other opportunities I have taken advantage of over the years as a family practice physician to generate revenue as I grew my practice:

- Worked as a mobile physician doing home visits for disabled patients;

- Worked as a physician evaluator of disability claims;

- Worked as a hospitalist doing hospital rotations, both day and night shifts;

- Worked in sports medicine doing sports physicals for athletic teams;

- Worked alongside a chiropractor evaluating his patients for certain medical treatments;

- Worked with an insurance company to do evaluations of patients in their homes;

- Assisted a retiring physician who needed to take medical leave, but wanted to maintain a patient panel for his practice before he sold it.

So take the time and research your particular field of medicine to see what you can do in your spare time to generate additional income.

Invest in Your Community

Take the time to invest in your community. When we signed up to be physicians, we all appealed to our altruistic natures, on some level, and the human need to serve others. Exercising this positive side of our personalities shouldn't stop once we start practicing as professionals. I conducted a short survey prior to writing this book, asking physicians if they volunteered in their communities. Forty-four percent said that they did not have the time to volunteer. It may seem counterintuitive, but the more you volunteer, the more you will enjoy your paid work. By participating in health fairs, doing free health screenings, giving health talks to large groups or as a media personality, or participating in a medical mission trip to another country, I found myself appreciating what I do as a physician even more. Patients want to know that you are invested in them and in their lives. Patients don't want to feel like a statistic or a penny in your coffers. More importantly, in order to be fulfilled by what you do for a living, you have to have a greater purpose beyond the bulge in your wallet. Your legacy should reflect your dedication to helping others. You know, that phrase we put on our medical school applications: "I want to help people"; but it should not always have a price attached to the services provided.

It takes a special individual to choose medicine as their life's work. We have special gifts and talents that enable us to serve a diverse population in a unique way. We have been blessed with the power to facilitate healing and prevent disease. Don't take this power for granted. Let's use our gifts to uplift our communities and do our parts to end health disparities across the nation.

I want to leave you with a quote I found called the Five W's of Life.

- Who you are is what makes you special; do not change for anyone.

- What lies ahead will always be a mystery. Don't be afraid to explore.

- When life pushes you over, you push back harder.
- Where there are choices to make, make the one you won't regret.
- Why things happen will never be certain. Take it in stride and move forward.

Always be moving forward.

This wraps up Chapter 7 on starting your own medical private practice in your own spare time, i.e., becoming the ultimate Lunchtime Physician Entrepreneur! We have covered how to discover your "why," create a business plan, setup the business, and invest in yourself. We also discussed the wide variety of available insurance plans and how to get paid, the intricacies of medical billing and coding, and unconventional ways to generate capital. That's a lot of information, right? What an amazing ride! I pray that you take these lessons and move forward to establish your own practice in your own communities. I have faith in each and every one of you. I did it, and so can you. I look forward to hearing all of your success stories, achievements, and accomplished goals. Don't be a stranger; I'm here to help you along through this process. You are not doing this alone, and your journey does not end here. Make every step count.

About the Author

Dr. Shanicka Scarbrough is a practicing telemedicine physician, entrepreneur, pastor's wife, dog mom, and leader in the Sacramento community where she currently resides after a long history of community involvement in Chicago, IL, her hometown. Along with speaking, volunteering, and working in the medical field for years, Dr. Shanicka now adds published author to her list of impressive accomplishments.

After receiving a bachelor's in biology, and then later her medical degree, from the University of Illinois at Chicago, Dr. Shanicka became a board-certified physician in family medicine. Presently, she is affectionately known as America's Favorite Family Doctor as she currently holds medical licenses in 15 different states, serving a plethora of patients via telemedicine and virtual health coaching across the country.

In her spare time, she provides free health screenings for those with limited access to these resources, not only in her local community but looks forward to expanding her ministry to urban areas across the country as free pop-up clinics. Dr. Shanicka has served as a ministry leader at Salem Baptist Church of Chicago, and looks forward to leading the health ministry at BOSS Church in Sacramento where her husband, Darryl Scarbrough, is pastor. Dr. Shanicka enjoys international travel as well, lending her expertise and medical skills in medical mission trips to places such as Haiti and parts of South Africa. When not giving back to the community, she enjoys reading, taking care of her mother, traveling with her husband, and spending time with their three dogs.

To connect, visit her website at www.DrShanicka.com

CREATING DISTINCTIVE BOOKS WITH INTENTIONAL RESULTS

We're a collaborative group of creative masterminds with a mission to produce high-quality books to position you for monumental success in the marketplace.

Our professional team of writers, editors, designers, and marketing strategists work closely together to ensure that every detail of your book is a clear representation of the message in your writing.

Want to know more?
Write to us at info@publishyourgift.com
or call (888) 949-6228

Discover great books, exclusive offers, and more at
www.PublishYourGift.com

Connect with us on social media

@publishyourgift

www.ingramcontent.com/pod-product-compliance
Lightning Source LLC
Chambersburg PA
CBHW070055120526
44588CB00033B/1558